W9-AKN-469

SABRINA FAUDA-RÔLE
PHOTOGRAPHY BY DAVID JAPY

To Pam

From Cinders & Mom

AUG 1 7 2018

JELLO SHOTS

hardie grant books

CONTENTS

CLASSIC

FRUITY

SPARKLING

TWIST

GIN TO
42

SPRITZ
44

CRÉMANT
46

JÄGERBOMB
52

MOSCOW MULE
54

JUNE
56

WATERMELON
TONIC 48

BISSAP RUM
50

CUCUMBER DRY
58

GRAPEFRUIT
60

SCREWDRIVER
62

RED SMILE
64

BASIL
66

PALOMA
68

PERROQUET
70

HANDY GUIDE

GELATINE

We use gelatine sheets, rather than powder, which need to be soaked in cold water for 10 minutes, then drained. Gelatine is suitable for all fruits except pineapple, because the enzymes it contains prevent the gelatine from solidifying. So with pineapple we use agar-agar, which has to be heated with the rest of the ingredients.

FRUITS

Cut the fruit in half. Scoop out the flesh with a tablespoon or a melon baller, taking care not to damage or pierce the skin. To keep the fruit skins upright and stop the contents spilling out, put them into glasses or bowls depending on their size. Reserve any unused flesh for other uses.

THE COCKTAIL

Bring the non-alcoholic ingredients to the boil, then remove from the heat, add the drained sheets of gelatine, and stir them in. Add the alcohol and stir. For jello shots consisting of several layers, check that the previous layer is fully set before pouring the next layer on top.

FILLING TO THE BRIM

To fill the fruit skins as full as possible and prevent the liquid from overflowing, pour part of the mixture into the empty fruit skins, chill, then top up with the rest of the mixture.

ALCOHOL FREE

Substitute the spirit with water or fruit juice to make non-alcoholic shots.

JELLO SHOT EXPRESS

To speed up the setting, put the liquid-filled fruit skins in the freezer for 30 minutes, then transfer them to the fridge. But please note: this method does not work well with watermelons, apples, cucumbers, tomatoes or strawberries.

MEASURES

Note that 1 tablespoon is 15 ml and 1 teaspoon is 5 ml.

MOJITO
JELLO

limes
4

light soft brown
sugar 4 tbsp

white rum
80 ml (2¾ fl oz)

sparkling water
60 ml (2 fl oz)

mint
3 sprigs

gelatine
4 sheets

Soak the sheets of gelatine in cold water for 10 minutes. Cut the limes in half lengthways and scoop out all the flesh with a melon baller. Squeeze the flesh to collect 120 ml (4 fl oz) of juice. Put the sparkling water and lime juice in a saucepan and bring to the boil with the sugar. Remove from the heat. Drain the sheets of gelatine, add to the pan and stir until dissolved. Add the rum and a sprig of mint and leave to infuse for 10 minutes, then discard the mint. Pour the mixture into the lime skins and top with a few small mint leaves. Chill for at least 3 hours until set. Cut into quarters and serve chilled.

Makes 16 jellos
Setting time: 3 hours

PUNCH TROPIC
JELLO

limes
6

shop-bought
mango juice
100 ml (3½ fl oz)

ground cinnamon
1 pinch

shop-bought
orange juice
100 ml (3½ fl oz)

white rum
100 ml (3½ fl oz)

light soft brown
sugar 1 tbsp

vanilla extract
1 tsp

gelatine
6 sheets

Soak the sheets of gelatine in cold water for 10 minutes. Cut the limes in half lengthways and scoop out all the flesh with a melon baller. Squeeze the flesh to collect 2 tablespoons of juice. Put the lime, orange and mango juices in a saucepan and bring to the boil with the vanilla extract, cinnamon and sugar. Remove from the heat. Drain the gelatine, add them to the pan and stir until dissolved. Add the rum and stir. Pour into the lime skins. Chill for at least 3 hours until set. Cut into quarters and serve chilled.

Makes 24 jellos
Setting time: 3 hours

CUBA LIBRE
JELLO

white rum
100 ml (3½ fl oz)

cola
120 ml (4 fl oz)

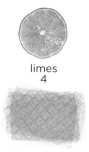

limes
4

gelatine
4 sheets

Soak the sheets of gelatine in cold water for 10 minutes. Cut the limes in half lengthways and scoop out all the flesh with a melon baller. Squeeze the flesh to collect 40 ml (1½ fl oz) of juice. Put the lime juice and cola in a saucepan and bring to the boil. Remove from the heat. Drain the gelatine, add to the pan and stir until dissolved. Add the rum and stir. Pour into the lime skins and chill for at least 3 hours until set. Cut into quarters and serve chilled.

Makes 16 jellos
Setting time: 3 hours

MARGARITA
JELLO

tequila
150 ml (5 fl oz)

lemons
4

flaky sea salt
8 pinches

triple sec
70 ml (2⅓ fl oz)

gelatine
4 sheets

Soak the sheets of gelatine in cold water for 10 minutes. Cut the lemons in half lengthways and scoop out all the flesh with a melon baller. Squeeze the flesh to collect 50 ml (1¾ fl oz) of juice. Put the lemon juice and triple sec in a saucepan and bring to the boil. Remove from the heat. Drain the gelatine, add to the pan and stir until dissolved. Add the tequila and stir. Pour into the lemon skins and chill for at least 3 hours until set. Cut into quarters, sprinkle with sea salt and serve chilled.

Makes 16 jellos
Setting time: 3 hours

PIÑA COLADA
JELLO

white rum
100 ml (3½ fl oz)

pineapple
1

shop-bought
pineapple juice
300 ml (10 fl oz)

coconut milk
180 ml (6½ fl oz)

agar-agar
3 g

Cut the pineapple in half lengthways and scoop out the flesh with a melon baller to within 5 mm (¼ in) of the skin, taking care not to damage or pierce the skin. Put the pineapple juice and coconut milk in a saucepan, sprinkle the agar-agar on top and stir well. Bring to the boil, then continue boiling for 2 minutes, stirring constantly. Remove from the heat, add the rum and stir. Pour into the pineapple skins and leave to set at room temperature for 2 hours, then chill for 2 hours until fully set. Cut into slices and serve chilled.

Makes 24 jellos
Setting time: 4 hours

LONG ISLAND
JELLO

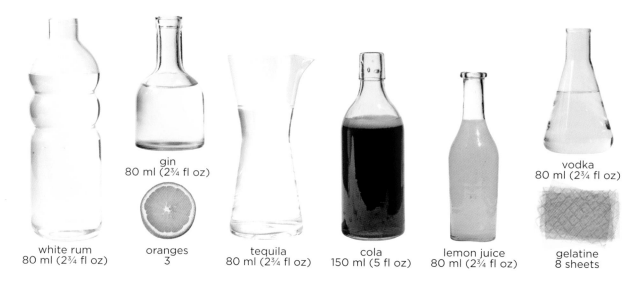

gin
80 ml (2¾ fl oz)

vodka
80 ml (2¾ fl oz)

white rum
80 ml (2¾ fl oz)

oranges
3

tequila
80 ml (2¾ fl oz)

cola
150 ml (5 fl oz)

lemon juice
80 ml (2¾ fl oz)

gelatine
8 sheets

Soak the sheets of gelatine in cold water for 10 minutes.
Cut the oranges in half and scoop out all the flesh with a
melon baller. Put the cola and lemon juice in a saucepan
and bring to the boil. Remove from the heat. Drain the
gelatine, add to the pan and stir until dissolved. Add the
spirits and stir. Pour into the orange skins and chill for at
least 4 hours until set. Cut into quarters and serve chilled.

Makes 24 jellos
Setting time: 4 hours

TEQUILA SUNRISE
JELLO

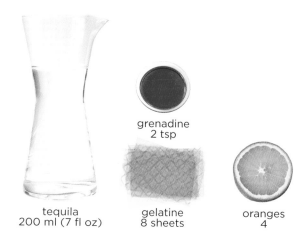

grenadine
2 tsp

tequila
200 ml (7 fl oz)

gelatine
8 sheets

oranges
4

Soak 1 sheet of gelatine in cold water for 10 minutes. Cut
the oranges in half and scoop out all the flesh with a melon baller.
Squeeze the flesh to collect the 400 ml (13 fl oz) of juice; top
up with shop-bought juice if necessary. Put the grenadine and
100 ml (3½ fl oz) of water in a saucepan and bring to the boil.
Remove from the heat. Drain the gelatine, add to the pan and
stir until dissolved. Pour into the bottom of each orange skin
and chill for at least 1 hour until the syrup has fully set. Soak the
remaining gelatine in cold water until soft. Put the orange juice
in another saucepan and bring to the boil. Remove from the
heat. Drain the gelatine, add to the pan and stir until dissolved.
Add the tequila and stir. Pour into the orange skins. Chill for at
least 4 hours until set. Cut into quarters and serve chilled.

Makes 16 jellos
Setting time: 5 hours

BLOODY MARY
JELLO

cherry
tomatoes
16 (80 g/3 oz)

shop-bought
tomato juice
240 ml (8¼ fl oz)

lemon juice
10 ml (2 tsp)

Worcestershire
sauce 1 tsp

celery salt
2 pinches

vodka
120 ml (4 fl oz)

Tabasco

basil
16 small leaves

gelatine
3 sheets

Soak the sheets of gelatine in cold water for 10 minutes. Cut off the top quarter of the tomatoes. Scoop out the inside of the tomatoes with a melon baller to within 5 mm (¼ in) of the skin, taking care not to damage or pierce the skin. Put the tomato and lemon juices in a saucepan and bring to the boil with the celery salt, Worcestershire sauce and 3 drops of Tabasco. Remove from the heat. Drain the gelatine, add to the pan and stir until dissolved. Add the vodka and stir. Pour into the scooped out tomatoes and top each tomato with a basil leaf. Chill for at least 3 hours until set. Serve chilled.

Makes 16 jellos
Setting time: 3 hours

STRAWBERRY DAIQUIRI
JELLO

limes
8

light soft brown
sugar 2 tbsp

white rum
100 ml (3½ fl oz)

gelatine
4 sheets

shop-bought
strawberry juice
200 ml (7 fl oz)

Soak 2 sheets of gelatine in cold water for 10 minutes. Cut the limes in half lengthways and scoop out all the flesh with a melon baller. Squeeze the flesh to collect 100 ml (3½ fl oz) of juice. Bring the strawberry juice to the boil. Remove from the heat. Drain the gelatine, add to the pan and stir until dissolved. Add half the rum and stir, then pour into the bottom of the lime skins. Chill for at least 2 hours until the syrup is fully set. Soak the remaining gelatine in cold water until soft. Put the lime juice in a saucepan and bring to the boil with the sugar. Remove from the heat. Drain the remaining 2 sheets of gelatine, add to the pan and stir until dissolved. Stir in the remaining rum, then pour into the lime skins. Chill for at least 1 hour until set. Cut into quarters and serve chilled.

Makes 32 jellos
Setting time: 3 hours

22 fruity

CHERRY CHÉRI
JELLO

lemons
4

basil
10 leaves

shop-bought
cherry juice
200 ml (7 fl oz)

gelatine
5 sheets

vodka
80 ml (2¾ fl oz)

Soak the sheets of gelatine in cold water for 10 minutes. Cut the lemons in half lengthways and scoop out all the flesh with a melon baller. Squeeze the flesh to collect 40 ml (1⅓ fl oz) of juice. Put the lemon and cherry juices in a saucepan and bring to the boil with 5 basil leaves. Remove from the heat. Drain the gelatine, add to the pan and stir until dissolved. Add the vodka and take out the basil leaves. Pour into the lemon skins, then snip the remaining basil leaves over the top. Chill for at least 3 hours until set. Cut into quarters and serve chilled.

Makes 16 jellos
Setting time: 3 hours

RUM PINEAPPLE
JELLO

pineapple
1

white rum
100 ml (3½ fl oz)

mint
12 leaves

shop-bought
pineapple juice
250 ml (8½ fl oz)

light soft brown
sugar 2 tbsp

limes
2

agar-agar
6 g

Cut the pineapple in half lengthways and scoop out the flesh with
a melon baller to within 5 mm (¼ in) of the skin, taking care not
to damage or pierce the skin. Zest 1 lime and then squeeze them
both to collect 100 ml (3½ fl oz) of juice. Put the lime and pineapple
juices in a saucepan and bring to the boil with the sugar, 6 mint
leaves and the lime zest. Sprinkle the agar-agar on top and stir
well. Return to the boil and allow to boil for 2 minutes, stirring
constantly. Remove from the heat. Add the rum and stir, then
remove the mint leaves. Pour into the pineapple skins, add the rest
of the mint leaves and leave to set at room temperature for 2 hours,
then chill for 2 hours until set. Cut into slices and serve chilled.

Makes 24 jellos
Setting time: 4 hours

CAIPRI PASSION
JELLO

passionfruits
10

lime juice
100 ml (3½ fl oz)

light soft brown
sugar 5 tbsp

gelatine
10 sheets

cachaça or
white rum
300 ml (10 fl oz)

Soak the sheets of gelatine in cold water for 10 minutes. Cut the passionfruits in half and scoop out all the flesh and seeds with a melon baller. Put the flesh and seeds in a sieve and squeeze to collect 300 ml (10 fl oz) of juice, topping up with shop-bought passionfruit juice, if necessary. Put the passionfruit and lime juices in a saucepan and bring to the boil with the sugar. Remove from the heat. Drain the gelatine, add to the pan and stir. Add the cachaça and stir. Pour into the passionfruit skins. Chill for at least 3 hours until set. Cut into quarters and serve chilled.

Makes 40 jellos
Setting time: 3 hours

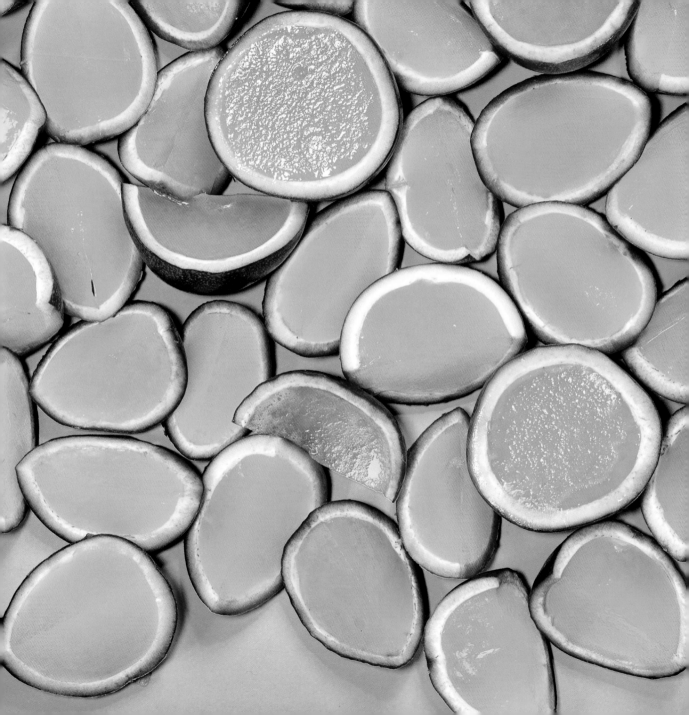

BIJOU
JELLO

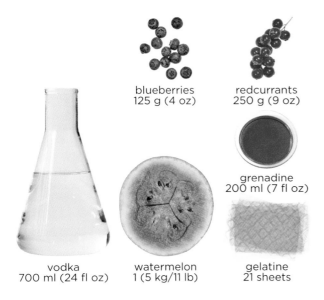

blueberries
125 g (4 oz)

redcurrants
250 g (9 oz)

grenadine
200 ml (7 fl oz)

vodka
700 ml (24 fl oz)

watermelon
1 (5 kg/11 lb)

gelatine
21 sheets

Soak the sheets of gelatine in cold water for 10 minutes. Cut the watermelon in half and scoop out the flesh with a melon baller, taking care not to damage or pierce the skin. Rub the flesh through a sieve and collect 1 litre (1¾ pints) of juice. Put the watermelon juice and grenadine in a saucepan and bring to the boil. Remove from the heat. Drain the gelatine, add to the pan and stir until dissolved. Add the vodka and stir. Pour into the watermelon skins and distribute the redcurrants and blueberries in equal proportions. Leave to set at room temperature, then chill for at least 6 hours until set. Cut into 32 slices and serve chilled.

Makes 32 jellos
Setting time: 7 hours

SAN FRANCISCO
JELLO

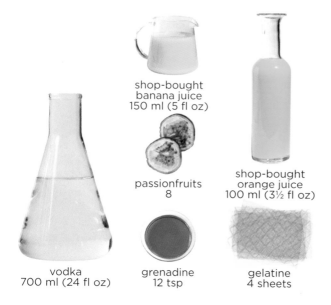

shop-bought
banana juice
150 ml (5 fl oz)

passionfruits
8

shop-bought
orange juice
100 ml (3½ fl oz)

vodka
700 ml (24 fl oz)

grenadine
12 tsp

gelatine
4 sheets

Soak the sheets of gelatine in cold water for 10 minutes. Cut
the passionfruits in half and scoop out all the flesh and seeds with
a melon baller. In a saucepan bring the orange and banana juices
to the boil. Remove from the heat. Drain the gelatine, add to the
pan and stir until dissolved. Add the vodka and stir. Pour into the
passionfruit skins and add a spoonful of grenadine to each one.
Chill for at least 3 hours until set. Cut into quarters and serve chilled.

Makes 32 jellos
Setting time: 3 hours

SANGRIA
JELLO

apples
4

triple sec
100 ml (3½ fl oz)

vanilla extract
2 drops

shop-bought
orange juice
200 ml (7 fl oz)

lemon juice
100 ml (3½ fl oz)

ground ginger
2 pinches

red wine
400 ml (13 fl oz)

port
100 ml (3½ fl oz)

light soft brown
sugar 2 tbsp

gelatine
4 sheets

ground cinnamon
1 pinch

Soak the sheets of gelatine in cold water for 10 minutes. Cut the apples lengthways. Scoop out the flesh with a melon baller to within 5 mm (¼ in) of the skin, taking care not to damage or pierce the skin. Put the wine, orange and lemon juices in a saucepan and bring to the boil with the ginger, cinnamon, vanilla extract and sugar. Remove from the heat. Drain the gelatine, add to the pan and stir until dissolved. Add the port and triple sec and stir. Pour into the apple skins and chill for at least 4 hours until set. Cut into 32 wedges and serve chilled.

Makes 32 jellos
Setting time: 4 hours

STRAWBERRY
JELLO

lime juice
10 ml (2 tsp)

strawberry
gummies
2

white rum or vodka
100 ml (3½ fl oz)

strawberries
250 g (9 oz)

gelatine
1 sheet

Soak the sheet of gelatine in cold water for 10 minutes. Remove the stalks from the strawberries and scoop out as much of the flesh as possible with the tip of a knife, taking care not to pierce them. Cut their tips slightly so they stand up, or put them in ice cube trays. Put the rum and lime juice in a saucepan and bring to the boil with the gummies. Remove from the heat. Drain the gelatine, add to the pan and stir. Leave to rest until the gummies have melted, then stir. Pour into the strawberries and chill for at least 2 hours until set. Serve chilled.

Makes 25 jellos
Setting time: 2 hours

BLUE BANANA
JELLO

tequila
80 ml (2¾ fl oz)

shop-bought
banana juice
220 ml (7¾ fl oz)

curaçao
50 ml

gelatine
4 sheets

lemons
4

Soak 1 sheet of gelatine in cold water for 10 minutes. Cut the lemons in half lengthways and scoop out all the flesh with a melon baller. Put the curaçao in a saucepan and bring to the boil. Remove from the heat. Drain the gelatine, add to the pan and stir until dissolved. Pour into the bottoms of the lemon skins. Chill for at least 1 hour until the curaçao has fully set. Soak the remaining sheets of gelatine in cold water until soft. Put the banana juice in another saucepan and bring to the boil. Remove from the heat. Drain the gelatine, add to the pan and stir until dissolved. Add the tequila and stir. Pour into the lemon skins and chill for at least 3 hours until set. Cut into quarters and serve chilled.

Makes 16 jellos
Setting time: 4 hours

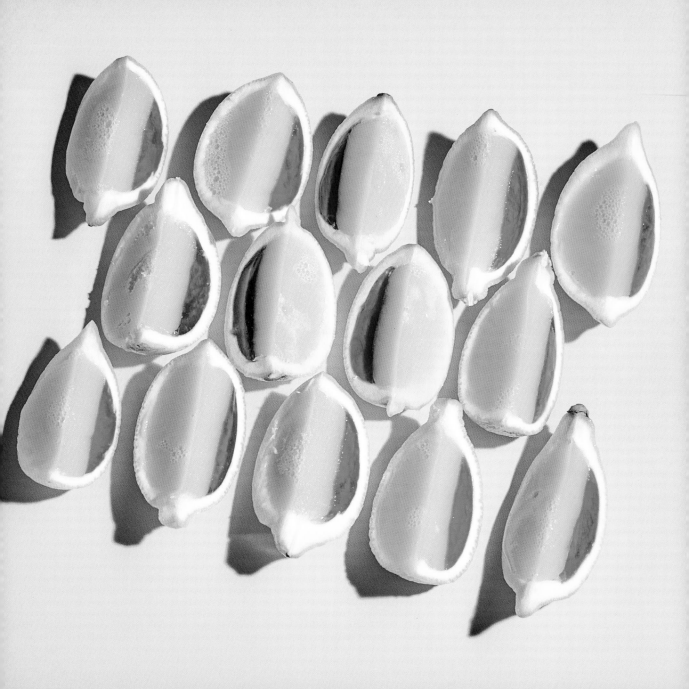

COSMO
JELLO

vodka
280 ml (9¾ fl oz)

clementines
8

lime juice
80 ml (2¾ fl oz)

Cointreau
120 ml (4 fl oz)

shop-bought
cranberry juice
120 ml (4 fl oz)

gelatine
10 sheets

Soak the sheets of gelatine in cold water for 10 minutes. Cut the clementines in half and gently extract the segments with your fingers, taking care not to tear the skin. Put the the cranberry juice, lime juice and Cointreau in a saucepan and bring to the boil. Remove from the heat. Drain the gelatine, add to the pan and stir until dissolved. Add the vodka and stir. Pour into the clementine skins and chill for at least 3 hours until set. Cut into quarters and serve chilled.

Makes 32 jellos
Setting time: 3 hours

GIN TO
JELLO

gin
100 ml (3½ fl oz)

tonic
150 ml (5 fl oz)

limes
5

gelatine
2 sheets

Soak the sheets of gelatine in cold water for 10 minutes. Cut
4 limes in half lengthways and scoop out all the flesh with a melon
baller. Put the tonic in a saucepan and bring to the boil. Remove
from the heat. Drain the gelatine, add to the pan and stir until
dissolved. Add the gin and stir. Pour into the lime skins. Chill for
at least 3 hours until set. Grate the zest of the remaining lime
and sprinkle over the top. Cut into quarters and serve chilled.

Makes 16 jellos
Setting time: 3 hours

SPRITZ
JELLO

oranges
4

Campari
160 ml (5⅔ fl oz)

sparkling water
160 ml (5⅔ fl oz)

gelatine
8 sheets

prosecco
320 ml (11 fl oz)

Soak the sheets of gelatine in cold water for 10 minutes. Cut the oranges in half and scoop out all the flesh with a melon baller. Put the Campari and sparkling water into a saucepan and bring to the boil. Remove from the heat. Drain the sheets of gelatine, add to the pan and stir until dissolved. Add the prosecco and stir. Pour into the orange skins and chill for at least 4 hours until set. Cut into quarters and serve chilled.

Makes 16 jellos
Setting time: 4 hours

CRÉMANT
JELLO

lemons
4

raspberries
16

vodka
50 ml (1¾ fl oz)

crémant
150 ml (5 fl oz)

light soft brown
sugar 2 tbsp

gelatine
4 sheets

Soak the sheets of gelatine in cold water for 10 minutes. Cut the lemons in half lengthways and scoop out all the flesh with a melon baller. Squeeze the flesh to collect 50 ml (1¾ fl oz) of juice. Put the lemon juice and vodka in a saucepan and bring to the boil with the sugar. Remove from the heat. Drain the gelatine, add to the pan and stir until dissolved. Add the crémant and stir. Place 2 raspberries in each lemon skin and pour the mixture over the top. Chill for at least 3 hours until set. Cut into quarters and serve chilled.

Makes 16 jellos
Setting time: 3 hours

WATERMELON TONIC
JELLO

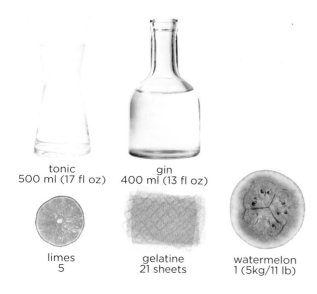

tonic
500 ml (17 fl oz)

gin
400 ml (13 fl oz)

limes
5

gelatine
21 sheets

watermelon
1 (5kg/11 lb)

Soak the sheets of gelatine in cold water for 10 minutes. Cut the watermelon in half and scoop out all the flesh with a melon baller, taking care not to damage or pierce the skin. Pass the flesh through a sieve to collect 1 litre (34 fl oz) of juice. Squeeze the limes to collect 100 ml (3½ fl oz) of juice; top up with shop-bought juice if neccesary. Put the watermelon and lime juices in a saucepan with the tonic and bring to the boil. Drain the gelatine, add to the pan and stir until dissolved. Add the gin and stir. Pour into the watermelon skins and allow to cool to room temperature. Chill for at least 6 hours until set. Cut into 32 slices and serve chilled.

Makes 32 jellos
Setting time: 7 hours

BISSAP RUM
JELLO

white rum
150 ml

limes
4

hibiscus flowers
1 tbsp

light soft brown
sugar 1 tbsp

gelatine
3 sheets

Soak the sheets of gelatine in cold water for 10 minutes. Cut the limes in half lengthways and scoop out all the flesh with a melon baller. Squeeze the flesh to collect 50 ml (1¾ fl oz) of juice. Put the lime juice, sugar and 100 ml (3½ fl oz) of water in a saucepan and bring to the boil with the hibiscus flowers. Remove from the heat. Drain the gelatine, add to the pan and stir until dissolved. Add the rum and stir. Leave to infuse for 10 minutes. Take out the hibiscus flowers and pour the mixture into the lime skins. Chill for at least 3 hours until set. Cut into quarters and serve chilled.

Makes 16 jellos
Setting time: 3 hours

JÄGERBOMB
JELLO

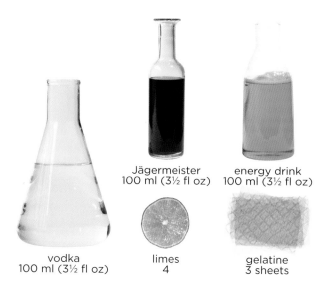

Jägermeister
100 ml (3½ fl oz)

energy drink
100 ml (3½ fl oz)

vodka
100 ml (3½ fl oz)

limes
4

gelatine
3 sheets

Soak the sheets of gelatine in cold water for 10 minutes. Cut the limes in half lengthways and scoop out all the flesh with a melon baller. Put the energy drink and the Jägermeister in a saucepan and bring to the boil. Remove from the heat. Drain the gelatine, add to the pan and stir. Add the vodka and stir. Pour into the lime skins and chill for at least 3 hours until set. Cut into quarters and serve chilled.

Makes 16 jellos
Setting time: 3 hours

MOSCOW MULE
JELLO

lemons
3

vodka
100 ml (3½ fl oz)

ginger beer
150 ml (5 fl oz)

gelatine
4 sheets

Soak the sheets of gelatine in cold water for 10 minutes. Cut the lemons in half and scoop out all the flesh with a melon baller. Squeeze the flesh to collect 50 ml (1¾ fl oz) of juice. Put the lemon juice and ginger beer in a saucepan and bring to the boil. Remove from the heat. Drain the gelatine, add to the pan and stir until dissolved. Add the vodka and stir. Pour into the lemon skins and chill for at least 3 hours until set. Cut into quarters and serve chilled.

Makes 12 jellos
Setting time: 3 hours

JUNE
JELLO

lemons
4

Malibu
100 ml (3½ fl oz)

coconut milk
50 ml (1¾ fl oz)

white rum
100 ml (3½ fl oz)

pomegranate
1

gelatine
4 sheets

Soak the sheets of gelatine in cold water for 10 minutes. Cut the lemons in half lengthways and scoop out all the flesh with a melon baller. Put the Malibu and coconut milk in a saucepan and bring to the boil. Remove from the heat. Drain the gelatine, add to the pan and stir until dissolved. Add the rum and stir. Tap the seeds out of the pomegranate with the back of a spoon to collect 40 g (1½ oz). Divide equally among the lemon skins, then pour the mixture on top. Chill for at least 3 hours until set. Cut into quarters and serve chilled.

Makes 16 jellos
Setting time: 3 hours

CUCUMBER DRY
JELLO

cucumbers
2 (250 g/9 oz)

lime juice
2 tbsp

vodka
60 ml (2 fl oz)

white vermouth
60 ml (2 fl oz)

coriander (cilantro)
3 sprigs

gelatine
2 sheets

Soak the sheets of gelatine in cold water for 10 minutes. Cut the cucumbers in half lengthways. Scoop and discard out the seeds and a little flesh to within 5 mm (¼ in) of the skin with a melon baller, being careful not to pierce or damage the skin. Put the vermouth and lime juice in a saucepan and bring to the boil. Remove from the heat. Drain the gelatine, add to the pan and stir until dissolved. Add the vodka and stir. Scatter a few coriander leaves onto the cucumbers and pour the mixture on top. Chill for at least 1 hour until set. Cut into 24 2 cm (½ in) segments and serve chilled.

Makes 24 jellos
Setting time: 1 hour

GRAPEFRUIT
JELLO

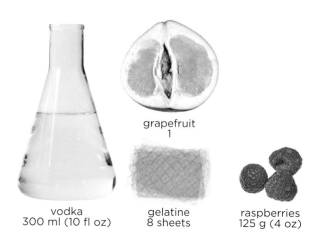

grapefruit
1

vodka
300 ml (10 fl oz)

gelatine
8 sheets

raspberries
125 g (4 oz)

Soak the sheets of gelatine in cold water for 10 minutes. Cut
the grapefruit in half and scoop out all the flesh with a melon
baller. Squeeze the flesh to collect 400 ml (13 fl oz) of juice;
top up with shop-bought juice if necessary. Put the grapefruit
juice in a saucepan and bring to the boil. Remove from the heat.
Drain the gelatine, add to the pan and stir until dissolved. Add
the vodka and stir. Scatter the raspberries into the bottoms
of the grapefruit skins and pour the mixture on top. Chill for
at least 4 hours. Cut into 16 wedges and serve chilled.

Makes 16 jellos
Setting time: 4 hours

SCREWDRIVER
JELLO

clementines
7

white rum
150 ml (5 fl oz)

gelatine
4 sheets

Soak the sheets of gelatine in cold water for 10 minutes. Cut
6 clementines in half and gently ease out the segments with
your fingers, taking care not to tear the skin. Squeeze the
flesh to collect 200 ml (7 fl oz) of juice. Put the juice into a
saucepan and bring to the boil. Remove from the heat. Drain
the gelatine, add to the pan and stir until dissolved. Add the
rum and stir. Grate the zest of the remaining clementine and
add to the mixture. Pour into the clementine skins and chill for
at least 3 hours until set. Cut into quarters and serve chilled.

Makes 24 jellos
Setting time: 3 hours

RED SMILE
JELLO

watermelon
1 (5 kg/11 lb)

strawberry syrup
250 ml (9 fl oz)

gelatine
21 sheets

shop-bought
strawberry juice
600 ml (20 fl oz)

lemon juice
250 ml (9 fl oz)

light soft brown
sugar 4 tbsp

vodka
400 ml (13 fl oz)

white rum
250 ml (9 fl oz)

Soak 5 sheets of gelatine in cold water for 10 minutes. Cut the watermelon in half and scoop out all the flesh. Put 250 ml (9 fl oz) of water and strawberry syrup in a saucepan and bring to the boil. Remove from the heat. Drain the gelatine, add to the pan and stir until dissolved. Pour the mixture into the watermelon skins. Allow to cool, then chill for 2 hours until the mixture is fully set. Soak 11 gelatine sheets in cold water until soft. Put the strawberry juice in another saucepan and bring to the boil. Remove from the heat. Drain the gelatine, add to the pan and stir until dissolved. Add the vodka and stir. Divide the mixture between the watermelon skins. Allow to cool, then chill for 4 hours until set. Put the lemon juice and sugar in a saucepan and bring to the boil. Remove from the heat. Soak the remaining gelatine in cold water until soft. Drain, then add to the pan and stir until dissolved. Add the rum and stir. Share between the watermelon skins. Chill for 4 hours until set. Cut into 32 slices and serve chilled.

Makes 32 jellos
Setting time: 10 hours

BASIL
JELLO

cucumbers
2 (250 g/9 oz)

basil
10 leaves

lemon juice
50 ml (1¾ fl oz)

Cointreau
200 ml (7 fl oz)

light soft brown
sugar 2 tbsp

gelatine
3 sheets

Soak the sheets of gelatine in cold water for 10 minutes. Cut off
one end of each cucumber and scoop out all the flesh with a
melon baller: twist the baller vertically like a screwdriver, removing
the flesh as you go. Stand the cucumbers upright in glasses. Put
the Cointreau and lemon juice in a saucepan and bring to the boil
with the basil leaves and sugar. Remove from the heat and discard
the basil leaves. Drain the gelatine, add to the pan and stir until
dissolved. Pour into the hollowed-out cucumbers and chill for
at least 3 hours until set. Cut into 24 rounds and serve chilled.

Makes 24 jellos
Setting time: 3 hours

PALOMA
JELLO

light soft brown
sugar 4 tbsp

grapefruits
3

tequila
300 ml (10 fl oz)

gelatine
10 sheets

limes
1½

Soak the sheets of gelatine in cold water for 10 minutes. Grate the zest of the lime half and squeeze the juice from the other lime. Cut the grapefruits in half lengthways and scoop out all the flesh with a melon baller. Squeeze the flesh to collect 450 ml (16 fl oz) of juice; top up with bottled juice if necessary. Put the grapefruit juice and lime juice in a saucepan and bring to the boil with the sugar. Remove from the heat. Drain the sheets of gelatine, add to the pan and stir until dissolved. Add the tequila and stir. Pour into the grapefruit halves, sprinkle with lime zest and chill for at least 5 hours until set. Cut into 48 wedges and serve chilled.

Makes 48 jellos
Setting time: 5 hours

PERROQUET
JELLO

pastis
100 ml (3½ fl oz)

gelatine
6 sheets

passionfruits
10

grenadine
5 tsp

mint syrup
5 tsp

Soak the sheets of gelatine in cold water for 10 minutes. Cut the passionfruits in half and scoop out all the flesh with a melon baller. Put the passionfruit flesh in a saucepan and bring to the boil. Remove from the heat. Drain 5 sheets of gelatine, add them to the pan and stir until dissolved. Add the pastis and stir. Pour into the passionfruit shells. Bring the grenadine and mint syrup to the boil separately. Remove from the heat. Drain the remaining gelatine, add half to each syrup and stir until dissolved. Gently pour the grenadine into half the shells and the mint syrup into the other half without stirring so that the syrup doesn't mix. Chill for at least 3 hours until set. Cut into quarters and serve chilled.

Makes 40 jellos
Setting time: 3 hours

ACKNOWLEDGEMENTS

With thanks to Delphine and my sister Alex, who have scooped out dozens of lemon skins.
With thanks to David for accepting this project, who has been a good
tester and who has put up with my messing around with Jello ;-)
And thanks to my tasters, testers and guinea pigs.

First published by © Hachette Livre (Marabout) 2017

This English language edition published in 2018 by Hardie
Grant Books, an imprint of Hardie Grant Publishing

Hardie Grant Books (London)
5th & 6th Floors
52–54 Southwark Street
London SE1 1UN

Hardie Grant Books (Melbourne)
Building 1, 658 Church Street
Richmond, Victoria 3121

hardiegrantbooks.com

All rights reserved. No part of this publication may be
reproduced, stored in a retrieval system or transmitted
in any form by any means, electronic, mechanical,
photocopying, recording or otherwise, without the prior
written permission of the publishers and copyright holders.

The moral rights of the author have been asserted.

Text © Sabrina Fauda-Rôle
Photography © David Japy

British Library Cataloguing-in-Publication Data. A
catalogue record for this book is available from the
British Library.

Jello Shots by Sabrina Fauda-Rôle

ISBN 978-1-78488-148-1

Photography: David Japy
Layout: Frédéric Voisin
Proofreading: Émilie Collet and Natacha Kotchetkova

For the English hardback edition:

Publisher: Kate Pollard
Commissioning Editor: Kajal Mistry
Desk Editor: Molly Ahuja
Publishing Assistant: Eila Purvis
Translation: Gilla Evans
Typesetting: David Meikle
Editor: Wendy Hobson

Colour Reproduction by p2d
Printed and bound in China by Toppan Leefung Printing Ltd.